WHAT'S WILD OUTSIDE YOUR DOOR?

PETER WOHLLEBEN

Translated by Jane Billinghurst

WHAT'S WILD OUTSIDE YOUR DOOR?

Illustrations by
Belle Wuthrich

Discovering Nature in the City

GREYSTONE KIDS

GREYSTONE BOOKS • VANCOUVER / BERKELEY / LONDON

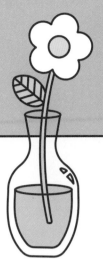

Contents

Nature Begins at Your Doorstep

I HAVE LIVED IN my home in the forest with my family and many animals for thirty years now. It's easy to see why I like writing books about trees and animals. But I lived in the middle of a big city for a few years when I was young, and I still visit cities occasionally. I love to find plants and animals when I'm walking down the street or waiting for a bus. Then one day I thought: I should write a book about nature in the city!

And so, I would like to take you on an adventure that starts right at your doorstep. You really don't need to go far to discover amazing things. Would you like to check out what's growing on the outside walls of your apartment building? Exciting things can happen even in your own room. I'll show you how you can grow an avocado tree and how to make your own compass. Or would

you prefer to raise a slime mold as a pet? As soon as you step outside, you can discover new things. Plants share cracks in the sidewalk with tiny creatures. Birds and bats treat high-rise buildings as though they were cliffs.

A lot of work went into the book you now hold in your hands. I spent many months working with Anja Fischer to make sure the text was clear and easy to understand. Then Jane Billinghurst translated it so you can read it in English.

But that's not all. A book about nature in the city with lots of experiments also needs photographs. But the photographer, Jens Steingässer, had a problem. How was he going to photograph lots of children when people could only meet in small groups because of the coronavirus pandemic?

Luckily, Eva-Maria and Thilo Schmid stepped up to help. They have a large family, and their children Juliane, Berenike, Helene, Charlotte, and Lasse were ready to try all the experiments I wanted in the book. Florin and Emilie are not in the photographs, but they helped set everything up. Even Leo, the family dog, joined in. And so, one sunny summer day, we took many of the photographs used in this book to show you how the experiments work.

Jens's daughter, Frieda, took our slime mold home and brought it back to life. Belle Wuthrich drew all the small (and large) pictures of animals and plants and put the text and images together beautifully so the book could be printed. Antonia Banyard spent a long time finding just the right pictures to add to this English edition.

Now that you know about what went on behind the scenes, would you like to start your adventure on your balcony, in your backyard, and in the city streets? Let's go! All you have to do is turn the page.

STAY SAFE

I'm going to show you lots of exciting things to do in this book. For a few of them, you need to take special care to keep yourself safe. It's a good idea to talk things over with an adult or two before you try them. And when you do, the adults might even want to join you in your adventures.

1
GETTING READY TO EXPLORE

GOOD SCIENCE IS BASED ON patient observation, whether in a laboratory or out "in the field," as scientists say. Most of the adventures in this book take place outside, so it helps if you know how to stay safe and prepared for the weather, how to observe wildlife respectfully, and how to preserve some of the treasures you want to bring home. Here are a few tips as you set out on your adventure to become a naturalist in the city.

Your Equipment

When you spend a lot of time exploring, it's good to know what to pack so you have everything you need close at hand.

YOU WON'T NEED all the things I'm about to mention on every trip. Often, though, you'll be more comfortable if you bring them along—which means you'll have more fun!

First, a backpack. A backpack is great because you can stash everything inside it and keep your hands free. It can hold a lot—a snack, binoculars, a jacket. If you're riding a bike and you want to get off, you can pack your bike helmet in there and keep exploring on foot. As you carry your backpack on your back, it's easy to lie on your stomach if you want to check out small animals and plants. And if your backpack is waterproof, you can go out exploring even when it's raining.

A small mat or cushion comes in handy on wet ground. Say you kneel on grass. Thousands of droplets of dew can hang on the blades—especially early in the day. Wet knees are uncomfortable, especially when it's cold.

A magnifying glass or loupe is a must-have. It makes everything larger so you can see even teeny-weeny specimens. If you want to examine a live insect, a bug box with a magnifying lens built into the lid is even better. Put the box on the ground and gently encourage the bug to crawl inside. Once it's inside, don't forget to check it out from underneath as well! When you're done, take the lid off and let the bug crawl out onto the grass.

DIVE DEEPER

• HELPFUL APPS •

Consider using the free app iNaturalist, which is run by the California Academy of Sciences and the National Geographic Society. You can take photographs and upload them to their website, where you can discuss your findings and experts can give you more information. Every observation helps scientists track changes in nature—even nature in the city!

If you're observing animals that are extremely shy or a long way off, you'll need a pair of binoculars. Perhaps you might get a pair for your birthday? Everything looks really close through binoculars. The higher the magnification, the better you can see the animals. But you don't want binoculars with more than 8× magnification. You can never hold binoculars completely still. If the level of magnification is higher than 8×, any slight trembling in your hands will also be magnified—and the image will wiggle so much you won't be able to see it clearly.

And finally, water is essential for exploration. Make sure your water bottle is full—and don't forget to pack a snack. Hungry explorers don't have as much fun. Some wet wipes or even a few dampened pieces of paper towel packed in a small plastic bag will help remove dirt or plant juices from your hands, but it's best to enjoy your snack before you handle plants and animals because you can't keep washing your hands when you're exploring.

STAY SAFE

Never look directly at the sun through your binoculars because you could permanently damage your eyes. And never watch a bird in flight through your binoculars. If a bird flies toward the sun while you're tracking it, you won't notice in time. It's much easier to watch a bird feeding on the ground or perching on a branch, anyway.

Be careful with hairy caterpillars like this banded woolly bear as their hairs can irritate your skin. This caterpillar will grow up to be a handsome Isabella tiger moth.

Keep Your Distance

A few animals can hurt you even though they don't mean to. Mostly, these are small creatures that are afraid of being another animal's dinner.

SOME ANIMALS, FOR EXAMPLE, defend themselves by biting or stinging if they feel trapped. Many give you a clear warning so they don't have to hurt you. They can't talk to you, of course. Instead, they warn you using an easily recognizable mix of colors—often yellow, black, orange, or red. Let's take a closer look at some of them.

The best-known animal with a do-not-touch-me pattern is an insect: the wasp or yellow jacket. The yellow-and-black stripes on its body warn birds and animals not to eat it. If they ignore the warning, they get a painful sting. Maybe that's happened to you at a barbecue or when you were eating cake at a picnic. Wasps, it seems, are easily upset. It doesn't take much and then they attack and pursue the animal—or person—they feel is threatening them.

DIVE DEEPER

• NATURE GUIDES •

A regional nature guide will help you figure out what spiders and snakes you might find while exploring. You can find guides online or at your local library.

It's best to remain calm and not swat at a wasp when it gets close to you. For people who are allergic to wasps, a sting could be life-threatening.

Like wasps, bumblebees' warning colors are yellow, black, and sometimes—depending on the species—white, but their stripes are wider. Something else is different too. Bumblebees are more laid-back. They sting only when a bird grabs them or you hold one tightly in your hand. You can get a good look at bumblebees in a park or in your backyard because they allow you to get quite close.

Then there are insects like ladybird beetles (ladybugs) that don't sting or bite but still send a warning message with their patterns of black on red, orange, or yellow. But why should ladybird beetles' enemies be afraid? When they feel threatened, ladybird beetles discharge a stinky fluid—from their knees. This liquid doesn't just stink. It also tastes bad—so bad that sometimes birds spit out ladybird beetles and never try to eat them again. Nothing will happen to you if you allow a ladybird beetle to crawl over your hand. If you close your hand around one, however, the beetle gets scared and then it begins to stink.

Other insects pretend to be dangerous. They cannot defend themselves against birds and other animals, but because they look dangerous, they are mostly left in peace. You can find some of them in your backyard or in the park. Hoverflies, for example, copy yellow jackets with similar yellow-and-black stripes, but you can easily tell them apart because hoverflies are smaller, and as their name suggests, they hover as well as fly.

You usually don't think of caterpillars as being dangerous. They have tiny mouths and no stingers—but stay away from the hairy ones. Some that look soft and cuddly have hairs that can cause a nasty reaction.

You may also come across spiders and snakes in town. Spiders are generally shy critters that don't bite unless they feel they have no choice, like when they are trapped in clothing or defending their eggs. Only a few are dangerous to people. Even so, it's a good idea to find out what spiders you are likely to meet on your expeditions so you know which ones are important to stay away from and which are harmless. Snakes, like spiders, would rather not meet people. If you see one, keep your distance and let it go on its way. It's not always easy to tell which are harmless and which are not, so it's best to be careful.

If there is a source of water nearby, you might find a garter snake. These snakes are not dangerous to humans and can be a real help in the backyard as they like to eat slugs.

Some plants, like this prickly pear cactus, have sharp spines to keep animals away.

Don't Touch Me!

Ouch!!

Plants don't want to be eaten any more than animals do, and so they find ways of defending themselves. Here are some plants you might find in the city that are very good at looking after themselves.

P LANTS NEED TO be even better at defending themselves than animals are. After all, plants cannot run away or fly off. They are rooted to the spot. One way they can scare off hungry animals is by hurting them. Have you ever been hurt by a plant? When you brush up against a stinging nettle, for example, your skin burns. The hairs on the nettles' leaves are like tiny syringes filled with acid. When they break off, their sharp points work their way under your skin, and the acid causes raised areas that burn.

Poison ivy and poison oak work slightly differently from nettles. Both contain oily resins that can cause an itchy rash. If you brush up against one of these plants,

wash your skin and anything you've touched with soap and water immediately to remove the sticky oils. If you live where these plants grow, this rhyme can help you remember what they look like: "Leaves of three, let it be."

Other plants have thorns and prickles to keep animals away. Straight or curved, they are sharp enough to prick you—and that can really hurt. Blackberry vines, for instance, are covered with prickles. If you try to walk through a blackberry patch, the vines grab your clothes until you can barely move. The prickles go through your pants or, if you are an animal, through your fur.

Another way plants defend themselves is with poison. Monkshood, which has a pretty blue flower, is one of the most poisonous plants that grows both in the wild and in flower gardens. All parts of monkshood are poisonous: leaves, flowers, and seeds. So please don't touch any part of them. One name for the plant is "goat's death," which makes it clear monkshood is very good at making sure animals don't nibble on it.

Many plants people grow in backyards or flower beds in public parks come from somewhere else in the world or have been bred for their scent or beauty. It's impossible to know them all—and lots of them defend themselves using poison—so don't touch a plant and definitely don't eat any berries unless you know for certain it's safe.

DIVE DEEPER

• POISONOUS MOUTHFULS •

The only plant monarch butterfly caterpillars eat is milkweed, which is poisonous. As the caterpillars eat milkweed, they become poisonous too. Then they turn into beautiful butterflies that make any animal or bird that tries to eat them feel distinctly unwell.

STAY SAFE

If you touch or eat something that might be poisonous, ask an adult to dial the number for the poison emergency hotline.

How to Preserve What You Find

If you find interesting animals, observe them, make notes about what they look like and how they behave, and then leave them be. If you find interesting plants, you can pick a few of them to bring home. Just make sure you aren't in a protected area and the plant isn't rare or poisonous.

FRESH FLOWERS WON'T KEEP for long, but there is another option: you can make your own herbarium. The odd name comes from the Latin word *herba*, which means "herb" or "grass." You won't preserve the whole plant for your herbarium—just a single stem with leaves and flowers. You press your specimen flat and dry it before sticking it onto a piece of paper. Then you file your specimens in a binder. The oldest herbaria in the world date back many hundreds of years.

SUPPLY LIST

YOU WILL NEED

Plastic bags

Damp newspaper

A small pair
of scissors

IF YOU'RE GOING ON a plant-collecting expedition, bring plastic bags, damp newspaper, and a small pair of scissors to snip the plants you want. Cut thick stems in half lengthwise when you get home. That way, the stems will lie flat in your plant press.

Find plants that are nice and fresh. Rare plants are protected by law and you can't pick them—not even in the city. You don't always know what is allowed and what is not, so here's a simple rule: pick only in places that are mowed. That could be your own lawn or a grassy area along a sidewalk. You can also pick plants growing in sidewalk cracks. Plant collectors make it a rule to pick just some of the plant and never the whole thing. That way the rest of the plant can keep growing. And don't just look for flowers. Leaves, like fern fronds, also look very beautiful when they are dried.

Wilted plants won't work well in your herbarium. If home is more than a couple of minutes away, put your specimens in a plastic bag. If it's really hot out, tuck them between layers of moist newspaper to keep them fresh.

Bring along a notebook and jot down when and where you picked the plant. Write down the area (for example, the name of the street) and exactly what the site looked like. You might have collected it from the crack in a curb or the edge of a pond or your own lawn. Note if the plant was growing in sun or shade. Plants fade as they dry, so record the color as exactly as you can or take a photograph.

STAY SAFE
Be careful of poisonous plants. If you've touched plants you can't identify, don't touch your mouth or your eyes. Wipe your hands with the wet wipes you brought along, and wash your hands thoroughly when you get home.

You've brought the plants home, and now it's time to dry them. If your specimens are wet from rain or from being between layers of moist newspaper, lay them out on a table to dry out a bit as you prepare your press. You can buy a press or your parents can help you to build one, but the cheapest and easiest method is to use a pile of books. You'll also need a few sheets of paper towel, pieces of cardboard cut to the same size as the paper towel, and a few pages from an old newspaper. I'll give you a tip here: use a regular newspaper because it will absorb moisture better than the pages from glossy magazines.

Choose a big book and lay a piece of cardboard on top of it. Put a couple of sheets of paper towel on the cardboard and then a sheet or two of newspaper. Arrange your plants on the newspaper, spaced as far apart as you want them to be in your file folder. Now cover them with another sheet or two of newspaper, followed by a couple of sheets of paper towel. Then put another piece of cardboard on top. Carefully place another big book on top. Finally, put a pile of thick books on top to make sure your plants get pressed nice and flat. If you buy a press or make one yourself, it works the same way. You don't need the weight of the books, because you tighten the press using screws instead.

Juices run out of the plants in your press the way juice flows out of a lemon when you squeeze it. If you have thick plants, you can change out the sheets of newspaper after a day. But if the stems and flowers of your plant are not very thick, you don't need to do this. All you need to do is wait. After a week or so, your plants will be dry and completely flat.

You can stick your dried specimens onto a piece of paper or into an exercise book. Scientists use a special kind of paper tape, but you can use a few drops of glue, a glue stick, or sticky tape. When you're finished, get out the notebook where you made your field notes. Copy everything you wrote about your plant onto the piece of paper. Perhaps if you check on the internet or in a book, you'll even be able to find out what your plant is called. The plants in your herbarium are now perfectly labeled and preserved.

Blossoms or colorful fall leaves make particularly lovely botanical art. After you have pressed your flowers, you can arrange them on a piece of paper around a poem. If you frame your artwork, it will make a lovely gift.

SUPPLY LIST

YOU WILL NEED

Plant press or paper towel

Cardboard

Newspaper

Heavy books

Glue or sticky tape

Notebook or sheets of paper

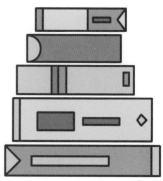

2
ADVENTURES
IN THE CITY

YOU HAVE YOUR BACKPACK. You know what plants and animals to leave well alone. It's time to pack your gear and head out into the city. Nature is everywhere! Come along and we'll see what we can find.

This peregrine is raising its chick high on a church tower in Lancashire, England.

Cliffs With Roofs and Windows

For many birds and bats, buildings in the city are nothing more than strangely shaped cliffs. And many cliffs make a mountain—with lots of places to rest and to nest.

Chimney swifts are found in eastern North America.

BATS LOVE OLD BUILDINGS. They sometimes squeeze through the smallest of cracks to get into attics. Once inside, they hang on to beams with their feet and sleep upside down until it gets dark.

Both barn and cliff swallows stick their mud nests under overhangs on the walls of buildings and on bridges. Tree swallows use nest boxes if there are suitable ones around. Look for swallows dipping through the air at dusk as they catch insects on the wing. Swallows are expert insect hunters and can carry as many as fifty live bugs in their mouths at one time.

Swifts are swallow-like birds that nest and rest on vertical surfaces such as cliffs or in hollow trees. In North America, Vaux's swifts and chimney swifts use tall chimneys as a substitute for big old dead trees in forests, which are becoming scarce. Once they find a chimney they like, flocks of swifts return year after year to nest and raise their young or to rest as they migrate south. Listen for the swifts' shrill calls as they circle overhead. You can tell swallows and swifts apart because swifts have a much longer wingspan, their wings are slightly bent, and their tails are stubbier. Chimney swifts depend on chimneys so much that as chimneys are gradually disappearing, so are the swifts.

Peregrine falcons are the fastest birds in the world, reaching speeds up to two hundred miles per hour (320 km/h) when they dive to catch their prey. Once endangered, peregrines are increasingly taking to life in the city, where they hunt for mice, which are plentiful in the city. They nest on bare ledges high up on buildings, where enemies cannot reach their chicks. Check to see if there are any cameras recording peregrines nesting in the city where you live. That way, you can track the chicks' progress from the comfort of your home.

In almost any city square or under any city bridge, you'll find rock pigeons. Although they eat almost everything—worms, fly larvae, berries, grains—they like plants best. There are few plants in public squares, so pigeons peck at crumbs from sandwiches or cookies instead. After all, bread and cookies are made from ground-up grain. They help themselves to leftover french fries too, which are made from potatoes— another vegetable.

Pigeons mill around, then rush in and grab any available food. The bravest will get quite close to you. In some cities, pigeons even land on people and eat out of their hands. Look at the tops of statues and buildings. If you see an array of narrow spikes, you know the city is trying to stop pigeons from landing there and covering the buildings and statues with their poop.

INSIDER INFO

• ADAPTING TO CITY LIFE •

Although peregrine falcons usually hunt by day, in cities they sometimes hunt at night, using the city lights to help them locate their prey. This is a good example of how city life can change how animals live.

DIVE DEEPER

• SLEEPYHEADS •

You can watch bats from the beginning of April until the end of October. Some bats migrate in winter, but most find a place to spend the season in a deep sleep. On their active days, the first bats fly as the sun goes down. As it gets darker, other species of bats join them. Streetlights attract moths, which makes them a great place to spot bats as they fly in and eat their fill.

Spare some ketchup?

Up High and Down Low

Many small mammals have adapted to life within cities. Here they are safer from predators than in natural areas, and there are lots of human food scraps for them to eat.

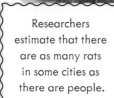

Researchers estimate that there are as many rats in some cities as there are people.

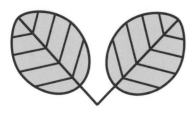

MICE AND SQUIRRELS climb plants growing up the outside walls of buildings, then store their food in attic spaces. People sleeping below are disturbed by the patter of little feet and the sound of nuts rolling around, which they usually don't appreciate. Instead of removing the plants, it's better to simply close the holes in the attic.

Check to see what color the squirrels are in your neighborhood. Most city squirrels are red or gray, but in some cities—Vancouver and Ottawa in Canada, for instance—they can also be black. In some states and provinces, you might find larger, reddish fox squirrels bounding from tree to tree. Check trees for cavities and leafy nests in forks between tree branches—places where squirrels like to nap and raise their young. A pile of the inedible parts of pine or spruce cones under a tree is a sure sign that a squirrel recently ate its lunch there.

Another bold climber and noisy attic dweller you might find in the city is the raccoon. In the wild, raccoons use their handlike paws to feel for crayfish and other small prey in ponds and streams. In cities, they like to raid garbage bins and dumpsters—and they can make quite a mess! Raccoons also enjoy fruit and often "harvest" it from backyards. Raccoons may look cute, but they can go on the attack if they feel threatened, so it's best not to get too close to them.

There's also a lot of life in pipes and tunnels underground. The dirty water from bathtubs, toilets, and dishwashers has to go somewhere or your house would fill with water. When you flush the toilet, the water rushes through pipes in your house and out into the sewer. The dirty water then goes out to a wastewater treatment plant.

Many animals have settled in sewers, including rats. Rats are very intelligent animals. In many ways they are much like us. They are ticklish and they dream. Rats even like the same food we do, although they don't mind if it stinks! They are happy to eat all the food scraps we throw away—preferably right off the compost pile. If they are really hungry, they'll eat the bits of food floating in water from the dishwasher, even when they are mixed in with water from the toilet.

Lots of people are afraid of rats. They used to carry life-threatening diseases, but most of these diseases no longer exist, and these days rats are no more dangerous than all the other wild animals in the city. Even so, they can be a nuisance, because they dig tunnels under sewers. This damages the sewer lines. That is why rats in cities are often poisoned. If you put food scraps in the bins provided for this purpose by the waste management departments of some cities, they won't end up on open compost piles or down kitchen drains. When there's no food, rats move to places where people don't bother them: back out in nature.

DIVE DEEPER

• COMPOSTING •

If you want to compost food scraps at home, you can purchase a rat-proof compost bin for your backyard or you can experiment with a worm bin in your kitchen, in your garage, or out on your balcony or deck. A special type of worm turns your kitchen scraps into lovely compost for your garden or potted plants. The technical term is "vermicomposting." You can find good instructions on the internet.

The City Excavation Crew

Some city critters dig holes, either to find food underground or because that is where they live.

. . . .

Pocket gophers can be super annoying when they dig holes in sports fields in city parks.

YOU ONLY HAVE to look at a mole's oversized front paws to see that it likes to dig. The mole uses those paws like little shovels. A typical molehill looks like a small volcano. The entryway is in the middle because as it digs, a mole pushes soil up with its head—and then the soil tumbles evenly in all directions. A mole excavates tunnels to travel along, chambers to sleep in, and places to store its food. A mole is small, but its underground territory is big: about half the size of a soccer pitch. Here it hunts insect larvae, earthworms, and mice. Moles never nibble on plants. In fact, they protect plant roots from hungry mice.

Unlike moles, pocket gophers and voles are vegetarians. A pocket gopher mound looks a bit like a molehill except it is horseshoe shaped. A vole digs its tunnels just under the surface as it nibbles its way through plant roots underground, pushing the excess soil out with its hind paws to create a flat oval mound with the hole on one side.

City parks with their wide-open grassy spaces are a paradise for rabbits. Rabbits are easy to find because these furry creatures enjoy each other's company and often dig lots of burrows close together. Take a look to see if you can find round black pellets near the burrow entrances. That's rabbit poop.

Where there are rabbits, there will be larger animals that like to eat them. Coyotes prefer to stick to natural areas within cities, but occasionally you see them trotting down the road in the middle of the day looking for tasty rodents—and sometimes small pets like cats. Coyotes are naturally shy of people, so you will rarely find their dens. People often think coyotes are moving into their neighborhoods, but in most cases, the coyotes were there before the people moved in.

Foxes dig holes with entrances so wide a small dog can fit inside. You usually find their excavations on embankments, where the soil is easy to dig. If you spot spiderwebs over the opening or see grass growing on the scraped-out soil, you know the den is no longer occupied.

Groundhogs are large ground squirrels. They not only dig burrows but also climb trees. They are also called whistle-pigs (after their warning calls) or woodchucks—although they do not chuck wood. Woodchuck is a mispronunciation of their Algonquin name, *wucack*, which means "digger." If you live in southern Canada or the eastern states, you might see one of these chunky squirrels on the grassy margins of a highway. Keep your eyes peeled!

One animal that doesn't dig its own holes but likes to take over old rabbit or groundhog burrows is the opossum. Possums, as they are commonly called, also den in crawl spaces under homes and in log piles in backyards. They use their naked tails when climbing trees. Possums move slowly and are often, unfortunately, run over. They are our friends because they eat a lot of ticks, little critters that can carry nasty diseases.

INSIDER INFO

• A LITTLE SPEEDSTER •

A mole can move through its narrow tunnels with lightning speed. It runs along at a speed of about 2.5 miles per hour (4 km/h). That's about walking speed for you but fast for a small animal.

Squeezing Into the Smallest Crack

It's not just animals that adapt to city life. Some plants do too. To survive, however, they need to be tough—and small. I recommend you bring your magnifying loupe along on this expedition.

. . . .

When it rains, water seeps into the cracks in the sidewalk, which makes it possible for moss and other plants to grow there.

IT'S WORTH TAKING a closer look at the cracks where sections of sidewalk or concrete don't quite meet, because plants often grow there. It's not easy for them in such a small space with not much soil. And when the sun heats up the concrete, it's hot and dry for the plants too. Only the toughest plants survive, and they are often very small. Let's see what you might find.

There's one that shines silvery green after a long dry period. It's easy to see how it got its name: silvery thread moss. The threads look a bit like little worms. This is the moss you are most likely to find in the city. It probably first grew on warm, dry cliffs where seabirds nest. No wonder it feels at home in the city. Hot, dry sidewalks are like cliffs—only flat.

Seabirds, like all birds, poop a lot, which is fine with silvery thread moss. Bird poop contains many valuable nutrients, including nitrogen. Nitrogen is plant food and helps plants grow more quickly. In fact, bird poop (packaged as guano) is often sold as organic plant fertilizer.

But where does moss growing on sidewalks find food? After all, the sidewalk isn't covered in bird poop (thank goodness!). The answer to this puzzle is car exhaust, which contains a lot of nitrogen. Rain washes exhaust particles from the air into sidewalk cracks. And so, cars fertilize plants. And that is why silvery thread moss is just as happy in the city as it is on the cliffs where seabirds nest.

Pearlwort

Dandelion

Broad-leaved plantain

INSIDER INFO

• TOO MUCH OF A GOOD THING •

The particles from car exhaust are blown into the forests outside the city. Trees like life in the slow lane, and the fertilizer in car exhaust makes them grow quickly. Unfortunately, trees that grow too fast don't live as long as they should.

A second tiny spreading plant you'll find growing in cracks is pearlwort. It looks a bit like a moss except it blooms. Its yellowish-white flowers usually have four petals. Even though pearlwort is small, it is an important source of food for bees and other insects.

The salt that is strewn over icy sidewalks in some cities dries out most plants, but pearlwort survives. When the other plants die, it has more space to spread. Like silvery thread moss, pearlwort likes nitrogen and so it doesn't mind car exhaust.

You also find crack-dwelling plants that would grow much larger if they had more space. Take dandelions. The ones in cracks are small, because people are always stepping on them. Sometimes the flower sits directly above the leaves instead of on a long stem like it would in a meadow. A narrow crack doesn't allow for deep roots, but sidewalk dandelions get enough food thanks, once again, to cars.

Broad-leaved plantain is another common plant in cities. It also doesn't mind too much if people step on it, and like pearlwort, it tolerates salt. When it grows outside the city, it gets much bigger and you can gather its leaves. If you get stung by an insect or a nettle, you can rub plantain leaves until they release their juices, then apply them to the sting. It will help take the pain away. But don't pick the leaves from sidewalk plants as they will be dirty from so much foot traffic.

Scent Mapping

There are a lot of scents to track down in backyards, in parks, and along the city streets. Why not put your nose to use and take a scent walk in the city?

DIVE DEEPER

• NAME THAT SCENT! •

Smell is tied closely to memory. Find plants with different scents. Pick a few blossoms or leaves and put them in small containers. Ask your friends to shut their eyes and remove the lids of the containers, smelling them one by one. What do the aromas remind them of? Different people will have different things to say about the same smell. They get bonus points if they can also identify the plant.

FLOWERS ATTRACT BEES and other insects with their scent. It's as if they're saying, "Come over here and sip my delicious nectar." Nectar is sugar water. Flowers offer it so bees visit and pollinate them. Some flowers with a weak scent or no scent at all during the day release their perfume at night. Night-scented stock and evening primrose, as their names suggest, are two such plants. Night-blooming plants can be important sources of food for moths, which sleep during the day.

These European orange-tip butterflies are flying early in the evening to sip nectar from night-blooming honesty.

Fruits such as apples or strawberries also smell sweet. This is to attract animals to eat the fruit. Then the animals poop out the seeds, and new apple trees or strawberry plants grow where the seeds fall, surrounded by a convenient package of fertilizer.

Trees have all kinds of different smells. Many are messages the trees send to each other. Trees use them to warn other trees of dangers—like bark beetles, for instance. You can only have a conversation when you're awake, and trees are the same. You can smell their messages only when it's warm and they're growing leaves, flowers, or fruit. If you stand under spruce or pine trees on a hot summer's day, the air will smell of resin and other tangy things. Most conifers don't like being hot, so the messages they're exchanging are probably not happy ones. But their messages smell good to us.

Grasses also warn each other of danger. For example, if cows or caterpillars come along and start nibbling, grass gives off a scent to try to drive off the animals and warn the rest of the grass that something dangerous is out there. You often smell this scent in summer when someone is mowing their lawn. I really like this smell. But the grass thinks an animal is eating it. And so, it tries to get rid of the lawn mower by releasing this scent—which, of course, doesn't work.

An even more common scent for you might be the smell of rain. How can that be when water has no smell? When raindrops hit the ground, the water that splashes back up into the air contains particles of mud. The smell of heavy rain is the smell of this mud. You can get this earthy smell even in a light rain. In this case, the smell rises directly from the damp ground, bringing with it the scents of fungi and decaying plants. Along the street, rain releases mostly dust from roads and sidewalks, so streets smell a little different from parks and backyards.

INSIDER INFO

• SCENT IN THE DARK •

Privet is a plant often used for hedges, and you can smell it only at night. Like many "nocturnal" plants, its flowers, which bloom in late spring and early summer, are white. That's good because like us, night-flying insects see white better than other colors when it's dark.

Female ginkgo
with fruit

What Stinks?

Not all outside smells are pleasant.
Animals large and small give off foul-smelling
liquids, and some trees and fungi really do stink.

TOMCATS LIKE TO mark their territory by spraying car tires with their urine. When a cat is doing this, its tail sticks straight up into the air and quivers. This scent marking keeps other cats away from its territory. If you walk by a car tire a cat has peed on, you'll know right away.

Lots of bugs release drops of nasty-smelling liquids when they feel threatened. Their names can clue you in. Take the green stink bug. It looks like a wide, flat beetle. Its smell lasts for a long time, so if you want to find out what it smells like, put gloves on before you touch one. Stink bugs love plant stems and fruit. If you eat fruit that doesn't taste so good, it could be that a stink bug got to it before you did.

Some trees smell really bad. Ginkgo trees have been around for the past 150 million years, longer than any other tree species on Earth. They tolerate salt, car exhaust, heat, and cold, which is why they are often planted in cities. They have one huge problem. Their fruit has a powerfully stinky smell. Like vomit—yuck!

There are male ginkgo trees and female ginkgo trees. Cities prefer to plant male trees so the trees don't produce any fruit. However, there are still lots of old female ginkgo trees growing in city parks and backyards. Look out for them in the fall. You will recognize the female trees by the nasty smell of their fruit. Some fungi smell of dead animals. The stinkhorn is one example. This mushroom uses its foul smell to attract flies and dung beetles. When the flies and beetles crawl around on the fungus looking for a rotting carcass, spores from the fungus get stuck to their legs—fungal spores are a bit like plant seeds—and so the fungus spreads. The insects are surprised when they can't find the delicious dead animal they are looking for. Stinkhorns can pop up in just about any kind of rotting organic matter overnight, so if you keep sniffing around, you might find one.

Skunks are shy and won't bother you if you leave them alone.

And, of course, we cannot talk about stinky animals in the city without mentioning skunks. Skunks like to den under decks. They are active year-round, and although they are mostly nocturnal, sometimes you see them during the day. They eat just about anything: birds' eggs, mice, snakes, mushrooms, fruit, and pet food. They also dig in lawns for insects and earthworms, and like raccoons, they rummage around in garbage.

When skunks want to defend themselves, they turn around and shoot out a really stinky liquid. They are good shots when they spray and can hit targets up to ten feet (3 m) away. That said, skunks don't have very good eyesight, so if you freeze when you see a skunk, it might just trot on past without even noticing you. You'll know if it's getting ready to spray because it will stamp its front feet, hiss, and arch its tail over its back. And if you have a dog, you really, really don't want it to get sprayed. It's almost impossible to get rid of the smell, and the spray hurts if it gets into your dog's eyes.

INSIDER INFO

• WHEN BAD SMELLS ARE GOOD•

Marigolds are slightly stinky. This makes them a great insect repellent. If you plant marigolds in among your vegetables, the food you want to eat is less likely to get nibbled by flies and caterpillars, which are kept away by the smell.

This male spring peeper is calling to mark its territory and attract females. The male who calls loudest is the one the females find most attractive.

Soundscapes

If you want to know what animals are around, it's good to listen as well as look. When people think about the sounds animals make in the city, songbirds come to mind, but you can hear lots of other animal sounds as well.

BZZZZ • BZZZZ

YOU CAN'T MISS hearing bumblebees because they buzz so loudly. As insects go, bumblebees are quite heavy. Their wings are small, and they have to move them quickly to keep themselves up in the air. That's what makes the buzzing sound. The sounds made by large insects like bees are low, while those made by small insects like mosquitoes are high. When a mosquito flies close to your ear, you hear an annoying whining sound—*tzeeeee*—that can keep you awake at night.

wow-wow!

Foxes bark at night mostly during mating season, which lasts from December to February. A fox's bark is a high, short, almost hoarse noise, *wow-wow*, that lets you know the location of the fox's territory. Coyotes also call at night. Their howls rise and fall, and they also make short yipping sounds. Coyotes call to communicate with one another and to defend their den or food.

At night, when the streets are quiet because most people are at home, you sometimes also hear strange shrieks. It sounds as though children are crying. But these aren't children, they're cats. Tomcats often have loud fights over territory. Both male and female cats yell in the spring at mating time.

You can sometimes hear something similar to the cats' screams during the day but from the air. Of course, cats can't fly, and so you need to look for a bird. Maybe you'll spot a hawk. When hawks are looking for small rodents on the ground, they fly in circles. They also like to eat roadkill, which is why you often see them perched on streetlights.

Have you ever heard a mouse squeak? Young people can hear them especially well because mouse calls are very high. The older people are, the less they are able to hear high-pitched sounds. The calls aren't loud, but then mice are small. You can often hear them in tall grass, where they are safe from their enemies. They call to warn each other if they notice a predator approaching. Male mice also "sing" when they're looking for females.

If you visit a pond or a lake in springtime, the frogs are croaking so loudly it's almost like going to a concert. Frogs croak by taking in mouthfuls of air and then letting the air out again. They pump in so much air, their throats (and sometimes their cheeks) puff out. Imitate the croak of a frog and see if any frogs answer and swim toward you.

DIVE DEEPER

• SOUND MAPPING •

Did you know there is a branch of scientific research called bioacoustics? Scientists record the sounds animals make in a particular habitat. That way, they can keep track of the animals even if they can't see them. Would you like to be a bioacoustic researcher and make a sound map of your neighborhood? Draw circles on a piece of paper. Mark where you are sitting in the center. Close your eyes and listen. Then open your eyes and fill in the sounds you hear. You can write the sounds down or draw what they sound like to you. How many of these sounds are made by people or machines and how many are natural? Does the mix depend on the time of year or the time of day?

INSIDER INFO

• BROOD X •

In 2021, trillions of cicadas from a group called Brood X emerged in the eastern United States after spending seventeen years underground. For four weeks or so, the air was filled with the males' high-pitched mating calls. There are many different cicada broods that emerge in the U.S. every thirteen or seventeen years. Brood I, for instance, will come out from underground in parts of Virginia and West Virginia in 2029.

Slimy and Smart

Blimey! I'm a slimy genius!

Fascinating creatures live in backyards and city parks: slime molds. As their name suggests, they are indeed slimy and they look a bit like mold, which is a fungus.

MANY SLIME MOLDS are yellow and spread over an area about the size of your hand. You find slime mold in moist places where dead wood is decaying. This could be under a hedge, on top of bark mulch or rotting leaves in your backyard, or on a fallen dead tree in the park.

All molds are fungi. But what are slime molds? Are they fungi, plants, or animals? The answer is none of the above. Plants make their own food. Slime molds cannot do that. Fungi break their food down and absorb it through their cell walls. Slime molds don't do that. Slime molds eat their food first and then break it down, which is what animals do. And yet, scientists are not ready to call slime molds animals.

Things get even stranger. Researchers have discovered that each slime mold is a single cell. One cell wouldn't be able to think, right? You can't have a brain if all you have is one cell. Even a fly has at least 300,000 brain cells.

Despite this, most slime molds can solve complicated problems. Researchers have tested them in mazes. In one experiment, they placed oat flakes—slime mold's favorite food—at one of the exits to the maze. Now all the slime mold had to do was find the shortest route to that exit. And, after a few attempts, it did exactly that. Wait a moment? Attempts? If you are to learn from a mistake, you need a memory or you would keep making the same mistake. And so, slime molds must have something like that.

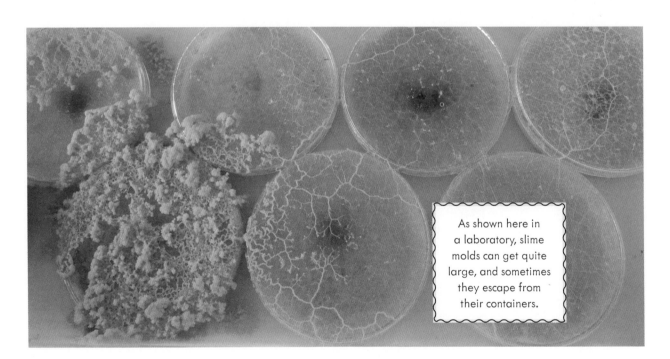

As shown here in a laboratory, slime molds can get quite large, and sometimes they escape from their containers.

ACTIVITY

SUPPLY LIST

YOU WILL NEED

A canning jar
with a lid

A sheet of paper
towel or a paper
coffee filter

Tweezers

Oat flakes

Access to an oven

A slime mold

The slime mold is on
the slip of paper in
the little plastic bag.

WHAT WOULD YOU THINK about having a slime mold for a house pet? It's a bit tricky, but you can do it with some help from your parents. First you need a container where your new pet can live. We placed our slime mold in a small glass bowl so we could photograph it easily. A canning jar makes a perfect container because you can pop the jar into the oven and set the heat to 210 degrees Fahrenheit (100°C). The oven will reach this temperature after about fifteen minutes. This sterilizes the jar before you introduce the slime mold to its new home. While the jar is heating up, have an adult pour boiling water over the metal lid to sterilize it, as well. Put the lid on a clean dish towel to dry and leave the jar in the oven to cool down.

Now you need a piece of coffee filter paper or paper towel cut so it fits in the bottom of your jar. You can use a clean oven-proof container and sterilize the paper and a few oat flakes at the same time as you sterilize your canning jar. Just keep an eye on the paper and the oats and take them out before they start to turn brown. It's best not to touch the paper with your hands. Use tweezers or a spoon to put the sterilized paper into the cooled jar to make sure you don't contaminate it with bacteria from your hands. Once the paper is in the bottom of the jar, moisten it with a few drops of tap water.

Now that your slime mold's new home is ready, where will you find a slime mold to occupy it? You have a couple of options. You might find one in your backyard or in a city park, but it's not always easy to tell what is a slime mold and what is not. There are many different kinds, and some fungi and lichen look a lot like slime molds. The easiest thing to do is to order your slime mold on the internet. Some suppliers sell only to schools, so you might want to see if you can make this a class project.

Add a few sterilized, cooled oat flakes to the canning jar to feed the slime mold. Use tweezers or a spoon. Then screw the lid on the jar so the moistened paper doesn't dry out. Open the jar briefly from time to time to let fresh air in.

Slime molds prefer to grow in the dark. You could cover the jar with a box. If you want to make a time-lapse video, just take the box off for a while.

Feed your new pet with a few sterilized oat flakes every two to three days. Once your slime mold has grown over the flakes, you can pick up a piece of it to give to a friend. Slime mold doesn't mind being broken up into smaller pieces.

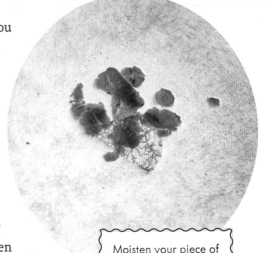

Moisten your piece of paper towel or coffee filter and put the slip of paper containing the slime mold on it.

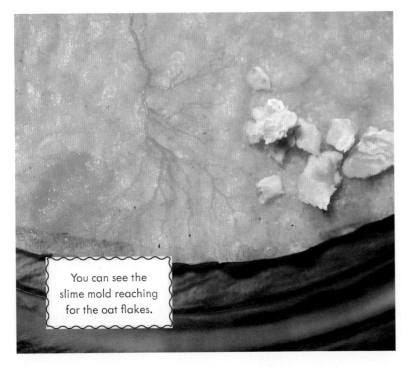

You can see the slime mold reaching for the oat flakes.

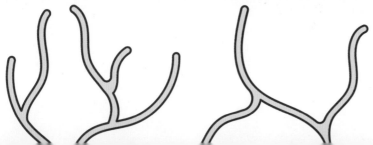

3
EXPLORING CLOSE TO HOME

EVEN IF YOU GO no farther than your neighborhood park, your backyard, or your balcony, there is plenty of nature out there for you to discover. Sometimes you can even bring nature into your own room.

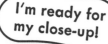

I'm ready for my close-up!

Hide-and-Seek With Insects

Insects are an important source of food for many different animals, including birds. Let's check some of them out. This is another expedition where it would be good to pack your magnifying loupe.

MANY INSECTS START LIFE as larvae or caterpillars, and a lot of these eat plants, so let's start by looking at leaves. Caterpillars nibble leaves from the outside in. Many birds hunt down caterpillars, especially when they have chicks to feed. Maybe you have seen busy little birds flying back and forth with caterpillars hanging from their beaks? As long as there are not too many caterpillars on a tree or bush, the tree will be fine and the birds will be happy because they have something to feed their young.

Caterpillars have various strategies to keep themselves safe from birds. Some roll themselves up in leaves so the birds can't reach them. Others weave webs where they sleep at night or feed during the day. How many caterpillar hiding places can you find?

Other tiny larvae feed right inside leaves to stay safe. You can see the wavy paths they make as they munch their way between the top and bottom layers of leaves. If you look closely, you will see that the pathway gets wider and wider as the larva eats and grows. These are the larvae of leaf miners, so called because as they make tunnels, they are "mining" their way through the leaves.

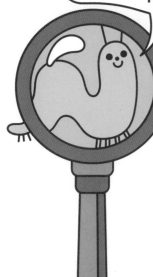

This leaf roller caterpillar has stuck the leaf together so it can feed safely inside.

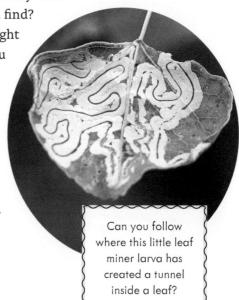

Can you follow where this little leaf miner larva has created a tunnel inside a leaf?

Another way to stay safe is to make your own private fortress. One insect that does this is the spittlebug. If you find a blade of grass with what looks like spit on it, what you are seeing is actually foam. If you wipe it away carefully, you'll find a small greenish bug inside, which is the nymph stage of the froghopper insect. Don't worry. If you're gentle, you won't hurt it and it will quickly make itself a new foamy hiding place. Eventually, the spittlebug will turn into a froghopper.

If you get down on your hands and knees—or even your stomach—you may find all kinds of beetles of different colors and sizes scurrying around, particularly at night. Ground beetles are on the hunt for other little critters they can eat. Admire them in your bug box and then set them free to continue their important job of eating insects that might cause problems in gardens and homes.

DIVE DEEPER

• "HUMMINGBIRD" MOTHS •

Hornworms feed on tobacco, tomatoes, and potatoes. If you see little white ovals sticking out from the caterpillar's sides, those are the cocoons spun by wasp larvae. The wasp lays its eggs inside the caterpillar. The eggs hatch and the larvae eat their way out of their still-living host. Hornworms that do not end up as a living larder for tiny wasp babies mature into large moths that hover in the air like hummingbirds as they feed on plant nectar.

INSIDER INFO

• POLLINATOR PATHWAYS•

Some cities have special programs to encourage people to plant flowers and bushes native to their area. These native plants provide places for local insects to feed and hang out. If enough people do this, then insects will find it easier to live in the city. Maybe you can check with your local conservation district or city landscape department to see if you can be part of a pollinator pathway where you live?

Spiders are not insects because they have eight legs, not six, but spiders do like to catch insects. To do this, they spin sticky webs. A great way to find spiderwebs is to look around outside light fixtures. Insects are attracted to the lights at night and spiders know this. Spiderwebs look especially beautiful early in the morning when they are hung with dew. If a spider spins a web near a window, you might be able to clearly see the creature's underside through the glass. The patterns and colors can be surprisingly beautiful.

This is the underside of an orb weaver in its web. Spider silk seems delicate but is stronger than steel.

Bald-faced hornet nest

Paper wasp nest

Wasps also prey on insects. Some wasps nest in the ground, but others construct beautiful nests out of paper that they make themselves by chewing on wood pulp. Wasps build their paper nests under the overhangs of roofs. At the end of the year, all the members of a wasp colony die except for the queen. She finds a safe place to sleep for the winter—maybe under tree bark or in a crack in a building. If you are lucky, you might find an abandoned wasp nest to examine. Paper wasp nests are flat with no outer covering so you can easily see the individual cells. Yellow jackets and hornets, which are similar to wasps, build cone-shaped nests with an outer covering.

Marmorated stink bug

DIVE DEEPER

• HUNTING DOWN SOME NOT-SO-NICE INSECTS •

Most insects are good, but occasionally insects arrive from other parts of the world and the local critters and plants don't know how to defend themselves against these new arrivals. You can have someone help you check to see if any of these insects are moving in close to where you live. Some, like the emerald ash borer, kill trees. Others, like the marmorated stink bug, can be a big problem for farmers and people who grow fruit. If you spot these invaders and report them to your local park authorities or conservation groups, you can play your part in helping control them. Maybe you can set up a competition with your friends to see who can be first to spot the intruders?

Emerald ash borer

On and in Your Home

Some small animals and plants can live almost anywhere. You might even find them on or inside your home.

Pill bugs are also called roly-polies because they can roll themselves up into a ball when they sense danger. Their hard outer covering protects them from predators.

ONE OF THESE CRITTERS is the pill bug. Pill bugs like things to be moist because they are related to crabs, crayfish, and shrimp, which are all crustaceans. Like fish, crustaceans can only breathe underwater because they don't have lungs like yours, but gills. And gills need to be covered by water all the time. That is why crustaceans die if they are out of the water for too long.

Pill bugs have gills, but you still find them on land. How does that work? The trick is that they suck up water and direct it to their gills. As long as they keep their gills covered with a thin film of water, they can breathe. Sunshine, however, quickly dries this film. So pill bugs like to hang out under bark, under rocks, under plant pots on your balcony, or under the mat by your front door. All these places are shady and moist—just what pill bugs like.

Earwigs often live close to people. The name doesn't sound very nice, does it? But it's not true that earwigs like to crawl through human ears to lay eggs in our brains! They use the big pincers on their flexible rear ends to catch small insects and to tuck in their wings. You don't have to worry about them pinching you because earwigs are asleep when you are awake. During the day, they hide in hollow spaces—for example, under rocks, bark, or in old plant pots.

Ants basically rule the world. There are ten million times as many of them as there are of us. Many like to live underground, moving crumbly earth up to the surface as they dig out their passageways to create anthills. Some live in rotting wood

Earwig

Ants often build their homes in the sand under paving stones.

(including rotting wood in buildings), and others burrow in soft soil under sidewalks, leaving tiny sandy mounds in the cracks.

Common black ants live in hollow spaces under rocks, in old wood, and even in cracks in walls. They mostly eat insects and drops of sugar water from the rear ends of aphids, but they will also help themselves to any sweet treats left lying around. Red ants can give you a nasty sting, so if you disturb them by mistake—maybe when you're moving a piece of old wood—step away until they have settled down.

Have you ever seen walls that are reddish or greenish in color even though the building is painted white? Algae are probably living there. Algae are tiny plants, and like all plants, they need water and food. When it rains, wind drives water to the wall. That's why you find most algae on the weather side of a building; that is, on the side where the wind usually blows. Algae also often grow on walls sheltered by trees. Trees sweat out a lot of water, which means the house walls are damper there than in other spots. The algae get their food from dust and exhaust fumes that get caught on the walls. So you could say that algae help to keep the city clean by purifying the air and turning pollutants into oxygen.

DIVE DEEPER

• FLAT AND GREEN •

It's easy to collect algae growing on the walls of buildings or on stones using adhesive tape. Take a piece of sticky tape and press it onto the wall. The algae will stick to the tape. Now press the tape onto a piece of paper, and look at it through your magnifying glass. Can you find different species of algae?

STAY SAFE

In southern states, ant-hills can be made by red fire ants, which have a painful sting. Be cautious around anthills if you don't know what kind of ant is living there.

Algae

You can make a delicious salad out of fresh dandelion greens. The leaves get bitter with age, so pick them when they're young.

Annoying but Tasty

Most people think weeds are a nuisance. But as they grow all over the place and some of them are even quite tasty, I think they are worth a closer look.

WILD PLANTS THAT GROW where they are not wanted are often called weeds. Weeds are not bothered by pests and diseases and grow pretty much anywhere. Gardeners pull them out so they don't get in the way of vegetables and flowers, but why not try a different approach? You can eat many weeds. "Wild vegetables" is a more attractive way of describing some of these plants.

Only eat wild vegetables from a home garden. Lots of dogs pee along the street and in parks—and their pee lands on plants. There can also be poisons in the ground. The plant roots absorb these, and if you eat the leaves and flowers, you will be eating the poison as well.

Unless you're a caterpillar, you're probably not a fan of nettles, because they sting. However, the tips that grow in spring are really tasty. It's best to wear gloves when you pick them and bring along a paper bag to carry them. If you cook them like spinach, they lose their sting and taste

STAY SAFE

Only gather plants you know well. And ask your parents to check in a book or on the internet to make sure you are collecting the right plant. If you're not sure, leave the plant alone.

Chickweed

really good. Just don't eat too many before you go to bed, or you will have to get up and pee a lot during the night.

Chickweed grows rapidly to cover everything. A single plant produces more than fifteen thousand seeds. The seeds are spread by birds and get stuck to the bottom of your shoes and then fall off somewhere else. Chickweed grows well just about everywhere, so you find it in most flower and vegetable beds. Pick whole stems with leaves and flowers. It tastes delicious cooked in soups and sprinkled on salads. It contains a lot of vitamin C, which makes it as healthy as some fruit.

Clover sometimes takes over lawns. It also grows in garden beds. That's great because you can eat not only the flowers but also the leaves, in small amounts. The flowers are slightly sweet and the leaves have a mild flavor. Pick a few petals from the flower head and suck on the ends. The liquid (nectar) inside is lovely and sweet. Clover is one of my favorite wild vegetables.

DIVE DEEPER

• SLEEPING WILD VEGETABLES •

When it's dark, chickweed goes to sleep just like you do. It shuts its tiny white flowers and brings in its leaves a little closer to its stems. Early in the morning and on rainy days are good times to observe this.

INSIDER INFO

• EDIBLE FLOWERS •

You can eat the petals of all roses, including wild roses. Sprinkle fresh rose petals on salads or freeze them in ice cubes. To freeze them, take small petals and wash them thoroughly. Fill an ice cube tray halfway with water. Place a petal in each cube. Freeze the tray. Take it out, fill each compartment to the top with water, and freeze again. You will have beautiful ice cubes to add to your lemonade!

The roots of white clover go as far as thirty inches (75 cm) underground.

Plants You Can Grow Yourself

You can harvest wild weeds, but how about growing some plants of your own? Some are edible and some are just for fun.

DO YOU LIKE EATING AVOCADOS? What about growing an avocado tree from seed in your own room? Take the seed of an avocado (also called the stone or pit) and wash it thoroughly to remove any flesh sticking to it.

Stick three toothpicks a little way into it. (Avocado seeds are hard, so you might need some help.) Use the toothpicks to balance the stone on a glass of water with the narrower end of the stone pointing up so it stays nice and dry. Now fill the glass until water touches the bottom of the stone. Put the glass in a dark place and top up the water every day. When the top of the avocado stone begins to sprout, move the glass into the light. Once roots have formed, fill your pot with potting soil and plant your seed. Place the saucer underneath the pot to catch any water that flows out when you water the avocado. You won't get any avocados from your little tree, but you will have a beautiful plant for your room.

SUPPLY LIST

YOU WILL NEED

Avocado seed

Glass

Water

Three toothpicks

Plant pot with holes in the bottom

Potting soil

Saucer

Maybe you'd prefer to grow something you can eat? Radishes grow fast and make great snacks. It takes only four to six weeks from the time the seeds sprout until the radishes are ready to harvest. Here's how you do it.

First, find a container. It should be at least six inches (15 cm) tall and have holes in the bottom so water can drain out. You could repurpose a large yogurt or ice-cream container. Just make sure you punch a few holes around the bottom and don't forget to put a saucer or something else—maybe a lid from a larger container—underneath to catch any water that flows out. The pot needs to drain because you don't want the plant roots to sit too long in wet soil or they will begin to rot.

Ask an adult for a bag of potting soil and carefully fill the container almost, but not quite, to the top. Then plant your radish seeds about as deep as the first joint in your pinkie finger. Leave enough space between them (about an inch, or 2.5 cm) so the plants have room to grow. Now put your container on a sunny windowsill, on your balcony or deck, or somewhere out in your backyard where it will not tip over.

INSIDER INFO

• NATURE'S WATERPROOFING •

Some plants, like nasturtiums, have waterproof leaves. When raindrops fall on them, the drops form small spheres that roll right off. The plant does this so that dust and dirt get washed away. It's called the "lotus effect" because it was first observed on a water plant called a lotus.

You can have a little herb and salad garden right on your balcony.

Stick your finger in the soil every day to see if it is still moist under the surface. If it's dry, add water. The first leaves will appear after a week. If you end up with two or more plants really close to each other, use a pair of tweezers to pull out the extras until the plants are an inch or two (2.5–5 cm) apart. Keep watering your radishes as they grow, or you will end up with long narrow roots instead of fat round radishes. They will be ready to harvest a few weeks after the first leaves appear.

If you don't enjoy the spiciness of radishes, you can grow lettuces instead. Sprinkle the seeds on the soil in your garden bed or in your container in early spring and cover them with a thin layer of soil. Keep the soil moist by watering it regularly. After two weeks, you'll see tiny lettuces starting to grow. If you're in a hurry, you can also buy lettuce seedlings and plant them instead. After your lettuce seeds show signs of green, you need to wait eight weeks before harvest. That's almost twice as long as radishes but still really fast.

If you wait too long, your lettuces will grow tall and skinny. Then they will flower and produce seeds. You can collect the seeds and keep them in an envelope in a cool, dry place and then sow these the next year. When lettuces grow tall stems like this, they become bitter and are no longer good to eat. So, if you want to eat them, you should pick them when the leaves are still close to the ground.

My favorite edible flower to grow is the nasturtium. The flowers are orange or red and insects love them. Bumblebees and other bees crawl deep inside to sip nectar. Both the flowers and the leaves are delicious and slightly peppery. When you pick the flowers, always leave a few so they can set seed. The seeds will fall on the soil, and next year you'll have more nasturtiums.

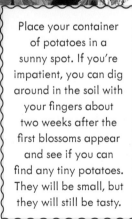

Nasturtium

Herbs are easy to grow both indoors and outside. Most grow really well in containers. Ideally, you want your herb garden as close to the kitchen as possible. You can grow a small rosemary bush in a container. Keep it outside in the summer, and if you live in a place where it gets below freezing for long periods of time, bring it inside for the winter.

Mint is best grown in containers because it can smother other plants in the garden. If you grow mint, you can harvest long stems with leaves and put them in a jug of water in the sun. Leave them there all day. Then take the stems out and chill your mint tea in the refrigerator. Delicious.

You can grow some vegetables without having to buy plants or seeds. Are there some potatoes lying around in your pantry? Perhaps a few of them already have some green sprouts growing on them and don't look that great to eat? Perfect. Let's get started. If you plant a potato in spring, you can grow a potato plant. Lots of new potatoes will grow underground—enough for dinner for the whole family. Potatoes take up a bit more space than radishes, lettuces, or herbs, but you can grow them in a vegetable bed, in an old plastic garbage can, or in a pot on your balcony.

Wait until it's at least 55 degrees Fahrenheit (12°C) outside. Then take your potato and cut it up so you have small pieces with a couple of green sprouts on each piece. Fill your chosen container with six inches (15 cm) of potting soil. Put the pieces of potato on the soil about six inches (15 cm) apart with the sprouts facing up and cover them with another inch (2.5 cm) of soil. For the next few days, keep the soil moist. As the sprouts grow, keep adding more soil so that only a couple of inches (5 cm) of green growth pokes up.

After a few weeks, when the sprouts blossom, keep watering your potato plants occasionally but stop adding more soil. Later in summer, the green growth will die and dry out. Now it's time to tip all the soil out of your container. Do this somewhere where you won't make a mess! Sort through the soil with your fingers and you will find a treasure trove of potatoes hidden inside.

Place your container of potatoes in a sunny spot. If you're impatient, you can dig around in the soil with your fingers about two weeks after the first blossoms appear and see if you can find any tiny potatoes. They will be small, but they will still be tasty.

— 4 —

WHAT YOU CAN DO TO HELP

ANIMALS ARE GOOD AT adapting and looking after themselves, but sometimes you can give them a helping hand by offering water, shelter, and extra food—especially in winter.

The inside of an old hedge is like a tunnel. Shy animals can walk through here without being seen.

The Secret Life of Hedges

If your backyard or local park is surrounded by a fence or a wall, birds can fly over them. But what about animals?

F ALL THE BACKYARDS and other green spaces in a city are separated by fences, many animals cannot wander freely to find food. There is, however, a solution to this problem that suits both people and animals: a fence made of plants. In other words, a hedge.

STAY SAFE

Don't eat fruit from hedges if you don't know exactly what they are. Lots of bushes growing in backyards come from countries a long way away. Some poisonous fruit looks similar to fruit that is edible.

A hedge is a row of bushes or trees planted close together. It's basically a green wall. No one can see in from the other side, and behind them you feel almost as private as in your own room. Animals love hedges. Birds can build nests hidden deep inside and raise their chicks without being disturbed. Foxes, hedgehogs, and squirrels use hedges like walkways. As long as they're traveling either in or behind the hedge, people can't see them. A network of hedges protects them and allows them to move around freely during the day.

A hedge is not only a good hiding place but also a good source of food, especially if the hedges are native plants. In spring, the flowers offer sweet nectar for pollinators. In summer, insects eat the leaves or suck plant juices. In fall, it's the birds' turn. Hedges produce berries that are an important source of food for many birds well into the winter. A hedge is particularly attractive if it's a mix of different bushes and trees. It not only looks beautiful but also produces many different types of fruit. Birds really like that—and mice, foxes, coyotes, and hedgehogs also snap up the sweet treats.

When hedges are left to grow the way they want, they can get quite tall and wide, especially if they contain yew or beech. If they are not pruned, they grow to about one hundred feet (over 30 m) tall—much too tall for your backyard. And so, you should cut a hedge back each year by the amount it grew. Then it will always be the same size. But when is the best time of year to do this? The trees and bushes in the hedge would prefer you to cut them back in summer. If you wait until fall, they will have fallen asleep and lost some of their leaves—and small cuts to their branches will take longer to heal. Nesting birds would prefer you to wait until fall. By then, they are no longer raising families and their chicks are long gone from their nests.

INSIDER INFO

• NATIVE PLANTS •

A native plant is a plant species that has grown in an area for a long time. It has adapted to local conditions, and local birds and insects have adapted to eat its fruit and leaves and enjoy the shelter it provides. If you want to attract wildlife to your yard or balcony, native plants are a good choice.

DIVE DEEPER

• LIVING BALCONY SCREENS •

You can even plant a kind of a hedge on a balcony. Small bushes work, but climbing plants require less space and soil. Ideally, find plants that will provide food and shelter for insects and birds in your area.

A woodpile is a good winter hiding place for insects. They creep into tiny holes in the branches or under loose bark.

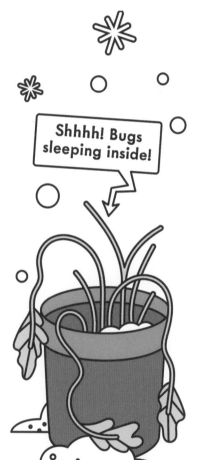

Shhhh! Bugs sleeping inside!

Safe Places to Hang Out

Life for animals is a constant challenge and sometimes dangerous. They need places where they can live and sleep safely.

SHELTER IS IMPORTANT in cold weather. Some animals sleep for many months. A sleeping animal cannot defend itself, so it looks for a safe, warm place where it will not be disturbed.

Small animals that need to keep their skin moist—salamanders and toads, for instance—seek out old, rotting wood. When it gets hot in summer and it doesn't rain for a long time, the little amphibians can hide in there without drying out. And when temperatures drop, moist wood doesn't get too cold. The best kind of rotting wood to hide in is a section of a dead tree trunk. You can often find sections like this where park trails have been cleared. Your local parks department can tell you where you're allowed to gather wood, and an adult can help you collect a section or two to take home with you to create a small woodpile.

Another great place for animals to hide is in a pile of leaves and twigs. If you have a hedge or bush on your yard that gets pruned every once in a while, you

In Europe, hedgehogs start to hibernate in November. You shouldn't disturb piles of leaves in your garden until they wake up in the spring.

can gather the cuttings into a pile. In fall, add raked leaves. Hedgehogs love piles like this. They sleep soundly and deeply all winter long.

Lizards look for piles of stones. In places where it gets cold, they hide in the nooks and crannies between the stones and sleep there for the winter. In summer, the stones warm up. Unlike toads and salamanders, lizards really enjoy sunbathing. After they've warmed up, they can run especially fast. That's important because lizards like to catch flies. And that only works if they are faster than the flies.

Many insects—tiny native bees, for example—need tall hollow plant stems to sleep in when it gets cold. Lots of weedy plants and grasses have hollow stems. If you don't cut them down, the stems dry out and stay standing through the winter. Because farmers mow most of their fields many times a year, it's difficult for bees to find somewhere to spend the winter. You can help. If you have a lawn, find out if you can allow part of it to grow long. Leave the dried grasses and other plants uncut until spring. When it's warm enough for the insects to fly again, this part of the lawn can be mowed again without disturbing the bees. Then just leave the grass to grow for the rest of the year.

You can also leave the dead plants in pots on your balcony. Insects can burrow into the soil, and bees can make homes in the hollow stems. Clean the pots out when the insects emerge and it's warm enough to plant new flowers.

Many people forget that birds and other animals need something to drink and like to take a bath every once in a while. In dry summers, birds often have to fly a long way to find water. You can help them by installing a birdbath in a spot where it's difficult for cats to sneak up on them.

Western fence lizards in the city have shorter toes for walking on flat surfaces.

All roses (except some ornamental varieties) form fruits called rose hips, which are an important food for animals in the winter, including this Bohemian waxwing.

Providing Snacks

Animals need to eat, just like you do. Out in the countryside they usually find what they need, but what about in the city?

Hang a container to catch seeds under the bird feeder. That way the feed will not fall on the ground, where it attracts rodents.

IF THERE ARE LOTS of trees, bushes, and flowering plants growing in backyards, parks, and abandoned spaces in the city where you live, animals and birds can nibble on seeds and fruit. Or they can catch insects or small animals scurrying in parks or between buildings. Some have even learned to live on what humans drop or throw away. Sparrows and pigeons patrol outdoor cafés for crumbs. Raccoons raid garbage bins for food waste. Mice dig rotting vegetables out of compost piles.

All this means that you usually don't need to feed wild animals in cities. But the situation is different in places where winter is cold. There are fewer food scraps because people are no longer eating outdoors and fewer plants in vegetable patches. Animals that are active in winter use up a lot of energy keeping warm, and many are grateful for extra food.

In places with cold winters, fill birdbaths with warm water once a day. It will remain ice-free for a few hours and then the birds can drink.

Sunflower seeds make a great winter snack for many backyard birds. You can also put out smaller seeds, oat flakes, peanuts, and raisins. It's best to put the food in a tube bird feeder with holes along its length. You can hang the feeder from a branch or a bracket attached to your balcony. The birds can peck out the seeds, and the seeds don't get dirty from bird poop.

If hummingbirds stick around in winter where you live, consider putting out feeders—as long as you will be around all winter to fill and clean them. Mix one part regular white sugar with four parts water. Bring the mixture to a boil to dissolve the sugar, and then let the sugar water cool. It will keep in the fridge for up to two weeks. Replace the sugar water in the feeder every three to four days. Red attracts hummingbirds, but don't add red food coloring because that can make birds sick. Instead use a feeder that has some red on it.

Whatever kind of bird feeder you put out, make sure you clean it with hot water and soap at least once every couple of weeks. Let it dry completely before refilling.

Have you ever wondered whether to feed birds in summer as well as winter? Even scientists don't agree about this. What is certain is that putting out winter food in the summer can be harmful. Chicks can suffocate on peanuts and sunflower seeds because they are so large, and sugar water in hummingbird feeders spoils quickly in warm weather. If you do feed in summer, choose different seeds and change out the hummingbirds' sugar water regularly.

Squirrels like to eat the same food as birds. If they visit your backyard often, you can offer them peanuts in their shells. They have fun nibbling the shells off with their sharp teeth. You can also buy special feeders with a flap that only squirrels can open.

5
NATURE ALL AROUND YOU

WOULD YOU LIKE TO KNOW why birds as tiny as hummingbirds and as large as these sandhill cranes fly south? Or learn how electricity flows in nature and light a lamp using a lemon? And just how does a compass work, anyway? Read on to find out!

You can see the trail from an airplane long after the plane has flown by. The tail of a shooting star is different. It lights up briefly, then disappears.

DIVE DEEPER

• **WHAT'S FLYING UP THERE?** •

Sometimes it's difficult to tell a satellite from an airplane. Here's how to do it. When an airplane comes closer at night, you can see it has more than one light and some of them are blinking. Satellites don't blink. Also, a short while after you see the airplane, you will hear the sound of its engines. Satellites are silent.

Sun, Moon, and Stars

Even in the city, nature is all around you: between buildings, on sidewalks, and under your feet. Most of nature, however, is far above your head!

THE SKY ABOVE YOU is a small part of an infinitely large universe. Earth is an even tinier part of it. We can't see much of the universe with our naked eye. Most objects are unimaginably far away—so far away that the light from many stars never reaches us. You can, however, observe a few celestial bodies. The most impressive one is the sun. The sun is an enormous star. It is so large you would need 1,300,000 planets the size of Earth to fill it. The sun sits in the center of our solar system, and Earth traces a path around the sun once a year.

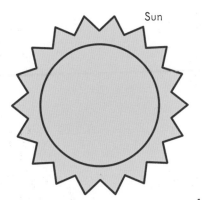

Sun

Earth

Moon

Every day, lots of bits of rock and grains of sand fly toward Earth from space. They pose no danger to us because they are traveling so fast they burn up as soon as they hit our atmosphere, which is what we call the layer of gases that surrounds our planet. You can watch this happening. It's a fun thing to do with your family or friends. Around August 12, wait until it's dark and then lie on your back on your balcony or in your backyard. Look up into the sky. If the night sky is clear, you will be able to see the Perseid meteor shower, one of the most impressive meteor showers in the Northern Hemisphere. At this time of year, as Earth is making its way around the sun, it crosses the dust trail of a comet. Up to thirty pieces of debris an hour burn up as they hit Earth's atmosphere. Each speck lights up briefly and leaves a short bright trail in the sky—what we call a "shooting star."

STAY SAFE

Never look directly into the sun with your naked eye or through a telescope or binoculars—that could cause permanent eye damage within seconds.

On a clear night, you can see many true stars, like our sun but much farther away, as tiny points of light in the sky. It's more difficult in the city than in the country because artificial light from buildings and streets drowns out the stars. Outside the city, you can see about five thousand stars with your naked eye. Inside the city, depending on the amount of light, you might only be able to see one hundred.

A more noticeable celestial body can be seen no matter where you are: the moon. It is a sphere made of rock that orbits Earth. It's about one-quarter the size of Earth. Even with your naked eye, you can see lighter and darker patches on its surface. If you use binoculars or a telescope, you can see individual features. There are mountains and valleys where the light and dark patches meet. You can tell them apart because the mountains cast shadows. The moon's many craters are also easy to spot. When a large rock flying through space hits the moon, the impact is like a big explosion that rips open a deep hole on the moon's surface. The largest crater is about three hundred miles (500 km) across, which is slightly wider than the Grand Canyon is long or about the distance from London to Edinburgh.

INSIDER INFO

• STARS, PLANETS, AND MOONS •

The sun is a star, and Earth is a planet. Both are large and round, but they are very different. The sun is a ball of fire so hot it shines brightly—like all the stars you see. Unlike stars, planets and moons are solid bodies that have no light of their own. The difference between planets and moons is that a planet orbits a sun and a moon orbits a planet. Our moon travels around Earth about once a month. The word "month" comes from the same word as "moon."

A sunflower likes to keep its leaves and flowers pointed toward the sun. Its stem turns during the course of a day, following the sun as it travels west. How does it do this? As one side of the stem grows faster than the other during the day, the whole plant turns toward the west. At night the other side of the stem grows faster, so by morning the sunflower is once again facing east—where the sun will rise.

Satellite

We say that the sun rises in the morning in the east and sets in the evening in the west. But the sun isn't actually moving this way. It is Earth that is turning around exactly once every twenty-four hours. From where we are on Earth, it looks as though the sun spends the day traveling in a big semicircle across the sky.

Out in space, stars, planets, and moons are all on the move—and so are satellites, which are human-made. Satellites do lots of things for us. Some have cameras directed at Earth. They fly so high they can see storms approaching much better than we can down here, and we use them to forecast the weather. Others measure the temperature of the air and the oceans to help us understand climate change. A few transmit television programs back down to Earth. If you want to watch these programs, you need a receiver on your house to catch the signals. You can see these receivers in many places: large round antennae made of metal and called, not surprisingly, satellite dishes.

On a clear night you can see satellites up in the sky. They look very similar to stars. Unlike stars, however, they move slowly and steadily. It's not difficult to find satellites at night as thousands of them orbit Earth. New ones are constantly being launched to do things like provide stronger signals for the internet, so you see more and more points of light moving through the sky.

If you live near an airport, here's a law of physics you can check out: light travels faster than sound. It travels at a speed of 186,000 miles (300,000 km) a second. Sound, in contrast, travels only about 1,100 feet (335 m) in the same amount of time. That's still fast: 750 miles an hour (1,200 km/h). No car moves that quickly, and most airplanes fly at only half that speed. Because sound travels more slowly than light, you see an airplane flying high in the sky before you hear it. The noise seems to come from somewhere way behind the airplane.

ACTIVITY

WOULD YOU LIKE TO use what you've just learned about the path of the sun to make a sundial? Drill a hole in the middle of a wooden board. (Maybe you can get someone to help you do this.) Stick an old pencil, a long nail, or a straight stick into the hole. Now put the board on a windowsill or out on your balcony or in your yard in a spot where it will get sun all day. The pointer in the middle will cast a shadow onto the board. Take a marker and draw a line to mark where the shadow falls every hour on the hour. Write the time on each line. As the hours pass, the lines you draw will fan out from the center of your sundial. On days when the sun is shining, you will now be able to tell the time using the shadows on the board. You never need to set this clock or change its battery. When the clocks change in the winter and in spring, all you need to do is adjust it by an hour. Or you could make a second sundial for the winter months.

SUPPLY LIST

YOU WILL NEED

A wooden board

An adult to drill a hole for you

An old pencil, a long nail, or a straight stick

A thick marker or pen

Thunder and Lightning

Have you ever gotten a mild electric shock when you were opening a car door? Ouch!

ACTIVITY

WHERE DOES THIS ELECTRICITY come from? You can do a simple experiment to help you understand what's happening. All you need is a balloon. Blow up the balloon and tie it off. Then rub it on your head. Do you see how your hair stands on end? That's because you charged your hair with electricity when you rubbed the balloon on it. The same thing happens to your body when you shuffle your feet on a carpet. You're rubbing your shoes on the floor just like you rubbed the balloon on your hair. The friction you create loads you up with electricity. This time the charge is stronger. You can feel the electricity leave your body when you do something like touch a car door—the shock might even hurt a little.

Friction is created up in the sky too. Water droplets rub up against each other as they drift around in clouds. When they do this, they get charged with electricity. There's a lot of friction in storm clouds. When the electrical charge is high, the electricity discharges, just like it does when you touch the car door. The discharge in a thunderstorm, however, is much more powerful, and you can see it clearly—as lightning that lights up the sky.

If you're outside in a thunderstorm, lightning can be extremely dangerous. It's safest to stay inside. But what if a thunderstorm arrives while you are out and about? Thunderstorms usually move very slowly and announce their approach with thunder, so you almost always have enough time to get inside a building. If you can't do that, never shelter under a tree. It's better to stay out in the open and crouch down. You'll be safest if you keep your feet close together.

INSIDER INFO

• CONSTANTLY CHARGED •

Electricity is flowing through you all the time. The current travels through your nerves. These are thin fibers that run all through you and carry signals from your brain to your body, and from your body to your brain. Before you move your feet, for example, your brain sends a signal through your nerves down your legs and to your toes.

ACTIVITY

YOU CAN USE FRICTION to make your own mini-lightning at home. You need a piece of clothing made from artificial fibers. A fleece, for example. Maybe you've already noticed your fleece sometimes crackles when you take it off at night. Turn out the lights and pull your fleece on and off. In the dark, you will see tiny bolts of lightning coming off your jacket.

Some animals use electricity. Bees, for example. A bee's wings beat the air as it flies, and the friction this creates loads the insect up with electricity. When the bee lands on a flower, a tiny electric shock passes from the bee to the flower. This changes the electric charge in the flower. The next bee that flies past can tell the flower has been shocked. It realizes another bee has recently visited and sipped up all the flower's nectar, and the bee knows it should fly to a fresh flower.

Young spiders also use electricity. When a spider wants to travel, it spins a long thread of silk from its rear end. A young spider is light enough that it can use this silk to drift through the air. However, the spider has a problem. The thread can easily catch on branches as the spider spins it, and if it does, the spider will not be able to fly away. And so, the spider waits for a day when the electric charge in the air is particularly high. Then the thread it spins rises up from its body like your hair does when you rub it with a balloon. Now the spider can launch itself into the air and allow itself to be blown away by the wind.

Electric Lemons

SUPPLY LIST

YOU WILL NEED

One lemon, perhaps two

A nail (which must be galvanized, which means covered in zinc)

A straightened copper paper clip or some copper wire

Regular wire (to wrap around the nail and the copper wire)

A small light bulb (a bulb from a bicycle light will work nicely)

ACTIVITY

DO YOU WANT TO TRY another electric experiment? Stick a galvanized nail partway into one end of a lemon and a straightened copper paper clip or a piece of copper wire partway into the other end. Wrap some regular wire around the nail and another piece around the copper paper clip or wire. Hold the wire attached to the nail to the metal threading at the base of the light bulb. Then touch the wire attached to the copper paper clip or wire to the gray dot at the bottom of the bulb. The bulb will light up!

Here's what's happening. As the acid in the lemon dissolves tiny pieces of the nail, electricity flows through these pieces of metal to the copper wire and then to the light bulb.

If one lemon is not strong enough, you can use two. This makes your battery twice as powerful. Just add a second lemon by sticking another straightened copper paper clip or a second piece of copper wire into the ends of both lemons to connect them. Have the galvanized nail with wire wrapped around it in lemon 1 and the first piece of copper wire (with regular wire attached) in lemon 2. Hold the ends of the two wires to the bulb as described above.

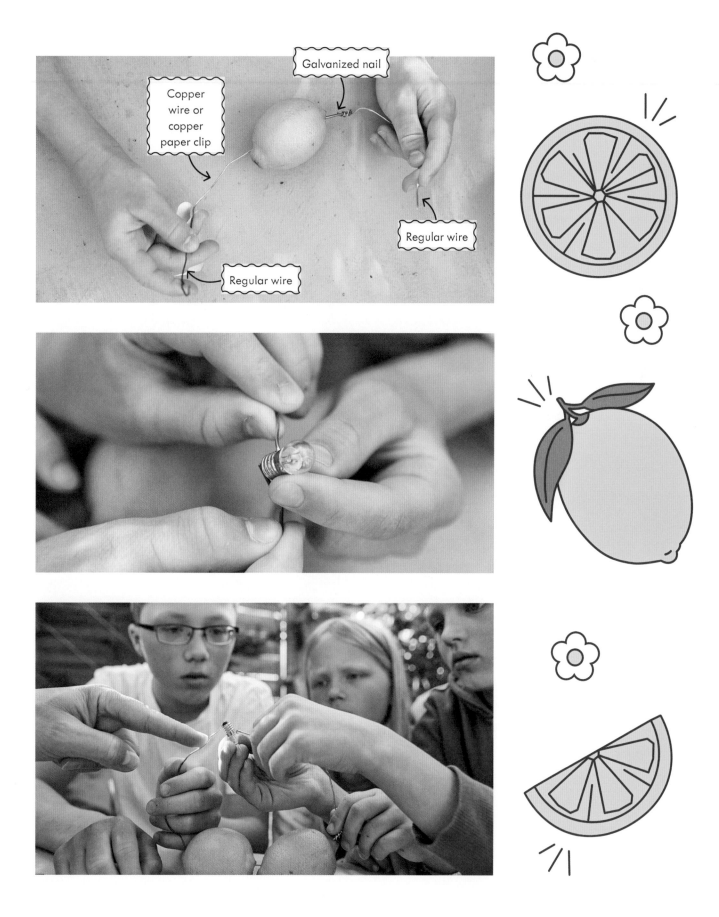

Without a Map or Navigation App

If you live in the Northern Hemisphere, every year in spring migrating birds fly back north after spending the winter in warmer places. How do they find their way home?

This swallow is on its way to Europe after spending the winter in Africa.

SUPPLY LIST

YOU WILL NEED

A cork

A needle

A magnet

Sticky tape

A bowl of water

SWALLOWS IN NORTHERN EUROPE fly south to Africa and return in spring. They fly over six thousand miles (10,000 km)—each way. Migrating hummingbirds in North America have the same ability to return to their nesting sites. These tiny birds fly as far as four thousand miles (nearly 6,500 km) each way when they migrate. Neither swallows nor hummingbirds have a cell phone with a navigation app. They don't need one because they orient themselves using Earth's invisible magnetic forces. It sounds complicated—and it is. Researchers have not yet discovered how it all works.

You are standing on the largest magnet of all: Earth. Not earth as in soil, but Earth as in our planet. Earth is an enormous magnet powered by its core. The Earth's core is about 4,350 miles (7,000 km) across and is a mix of solid and liquid metal. Magnetized iron is attracted to the magnetic North and South Poles. These magnetic poles are roughly where you find the geographic North and South Poles on a globe. This means you can use a magnetized needle to find north and south. Would you like to try that for yourself?

ACTIVITY

A COMPASS IS A TOOL that points north. You can make a simple compass yourself. Cut a slice off the end of a cork. Drag the sharp end of a needle over one end of a magnet about thirty times, always moving it in the same direction. That will magnetize the sharp end. Attach the needle to the slice of cork with sticky tape so both ends extend the same distance from the cork. Now float the cork in a bowl of water. No matter how you turn the bowl, the sharp end of the needle will keep pointing in the same direction—and so you can use the needle as a compass.

Birds that sense Earth's magnetic fields are a bit like your compass. No matter which way they turn, they always know which direction is north. They are orienting themselves to Earth's inner magnet. Other animals also have a magnetic sense. Salmon swim in the ocean and return to the rivers and streams where they were born to lay their eggs. This only works if they know exactly which river estuary to turn in to. Bees, mice, and horses all have a magnetic sense. Unfortunately, we do not. Instead, we rely on maps and navigation systems—or maybe a homemade compass.

Researchers are trying to find out where animals' magnetic sense is located. They have found tiny pieces of magnetic metal in animals' bodies. In pigeons, most of these pieces can be found in their beaks; in fish, most are in their noses. But it's not yet clear how this metal is connected to the animals' brains.

INSIDER INFO

• INTERFERENCE •

If you hold a cell phone close to the needle floating in the bowl of water, the needle will turn slightly away because there is a magnet built into the phone's speaker. As we have no magnetic sense, this magnet doesn't bother us.

DIVE DEEPER

• NORTH OR SOUTH? •

Every magnet has a north pole and a south pole. You can't tell the difference unless they are marked. If you charge the sharp end of the needle for your compass by dragging it over the south pole end of the magnet instead of the north pole end, it will point south—that is to say, in the wrong direction. You can easily check this using the sun. The sun always stands in the south at midday. If the charged end of your compass needle points away from the sun, all is as it should be. A compass that you buy always points north.

Anoles are North American lizards that can change color from green to brown depending on their background, the temperature, and their mood. There are many kinds of anoles in a wide range of sizes.

How Color Gets Into the World

Animals and plants come in many different colors. On sunny days, the sky is blue. But how is it that we see color in the first place?

THE SUN IS THE SOURCE of all the colors in nature. Its light looks white, but it's actually a combination of many colors. You can see that in a rainbow. Water droplets in the air split sunlight into red, orange, yellow, green, blue, indigo, and violet. Do you want to check this out? You can make your own rainbow at home.

ACTIVITY

PUT THE BOWL WITH WATER near a sunny window—or do this activity outside on a nice day. Hold the mirror in the water with one hand. With your other hand, hold the piece of paper next to the bowl so the light reflected from the mirror hits the paper. You will see a mini-rainbow with bright colors. It may not be a beautiful arc like a rainbow in the sky, but you will see the different colors.

If it doesn't work right away, gently tip the mirror back and forth until the colors appear. Are you wondering why this happens? The water and the mirror break the sunlight down into the colors that combine to make sunlight white.

Animals and plants—and all other life-forms and objects around us—reflect sunlight just as the mirror does. But they don't reflect all of it. If they did, every life-form and object would look white to us.

Colors in nature—and everywhere else—happen because all animals and plants absorb part of the light and reflect what is left. Therefore, you need light to see color. Without light everything looks black. You notice that at night when you turn out the light so you can go to sleep.

The leaves of plants absorb red and blue light. Plants use this light to get the energy they need to make sugar. They can't use green light, so they reflect it—and this is the color we see. Red petals absorb blue and green light, so only red light

SUPPLY LIST

YOU WILL NEED

A shallow bowl half filled with water

A small mirror

A piece of white paper

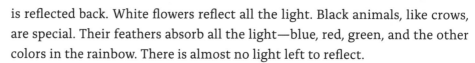

is reflected back. White flowers reflect all the light. Black animals, like crows, are special. Their feathers absorb all the light—blue, red, green, and the other colors in the rainbow. There is almost no light left to reflect.

Black surfaces, which absorb all the light, warm up very quickly. Black clothes get really hot in the sun, but white clothes don't heat up as much. That is why you'll stay cooler if you wear light colors on a hot summer's day.

Now let's consider why the sky is blue in good weather. When the sun shines, its light doesn't fall directly on the ground. It has to shine through the layer of gases (the atmosphere) that surrounds Earth. There, sunlight hits water droplets and other minute particles, which split it into many colors, like in our experiment with the mirror. Blue light ends up being scattered most widely and is therefore most visible.

It's a beautiful thing to see the world in color. It's also important for us and for many animals so that we can, for example, recognize ripe red fruit. That only works because we have little sensors in our eyes that react to red, green, and blue light. Quite a few animals, including dogs and their relatives, don't have sensors that react to red light. All they can see is blue and perhaps a bit of yellow. Some people think these animals will be able to see us really well if we wear a red jacket. But now you know. You are better camouflaged if you wear red than if you wear blue. And so, if you want to observe animals without them being able to see you, it's best not to wear a blue jacket.

If plants, animals, or people stay out in the sun for too long, their skin can burn. Color stored in the skin provides a bit of protection. Many apples turn red just before they ripen. The red color protects the apple from sunburn. If the sun isn't shining just before the apple ripens, it remains pale green. That's similar to skin. Darker skin is a natural protection from sunburn. Light skin turns brown in the sun, and after that it doesn't burn as quickly. If a light-skinned person often wears a T-shirt in the summer, their arms turn brown up to the sleeves and are much lighter above that. In those places that don't get much sun, white skin doesn't need protection. It's the same with red apples on a tree. The side facing the sun is much redder than the side that is in the shade.

• FLASHLIGHTS AND LANTERNS •

In the absence of sunlight, you can use flashlights or lanterns to create colors. Unlike the sun, light bulbs shine only one color. Green bulbs glow green, red bulbs glow red, and blue bulbs glow blue. If you shine them all together, you get white. That's how the screen of a smartphone works. It's made up of tiny red, green, and blue lights. Together these colors make up all the different colors you see. You can check out these tiny lights in your cell phone using a magnifying loupe.

ACTIVITY

DO YOU HAVE AN APPLE TREE in your backyard that grows red apples? You can experiment with decorating an apple still hanging on the tree.

Cut a heart out of an adhesive material that blocks light and stick it onto an apple in summer. You could also choose another shape—the first letter of your name, for instance. Stick the material onto the side of the apple that faces south. That's the side where the sun will shine on the apple longest.

Shortly before it's time to pick the apple, after the apple has turned red, take the heart off. The skin of the apple under the heart will still be pale green or yellow. You will now have a light heart on a red apple. The heart has protected the apple from the rays of the sun.

Many animals use colors to blend into a background or to stand out against it. If an animal wants to make itself invisible, the color of its fur, skin, or feathers must match its surroundings exactly. Weasels, for example, which sometimes slip into cities, are usually brownish, but in northern parts of their range, they turn white in winter. If the snow melts before they have had time to shed their winter coats, then predators can spot them right away.

INSIDER INFO

• THE DEEP BLUE SEA •

The ocean and some rivers and lakes look blue. Many people think the sky is reflected in the water. But actually, like leaves on plants, deep water absorbs colors. However, unlike plant leaves, deep water absorbs green and red, which leaves blue—the color we see when we look at the water.

Yellow clouds drift above conifers when they release large quantities of pollen.

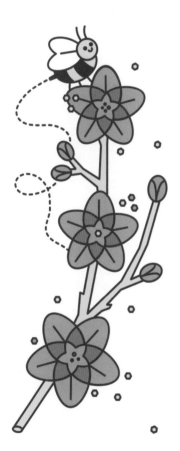

Covered in Dust

Cities are dusty places. Just take a look at car windshields when it hasn't rained for a while. But where does all this dust come from?

FOR STARTERS, THERE ARE TREES. Usually, if a tree is to form seeds and fruit, its flowers must be dusted with pollen from another tree of the same species. Pollen grains are tiny spheres you can barely see with your naked eye. Bees transfer pollen grains when they fly from tree to tree. They sip nectar from flowers, and as they do so, pollen grains on little stalks next to the drops of nectar get stuck to the hairs on their body. You can watch bees hard at work in the blossoms of apple and cherry trees.

For many trees, however, pollination happens without the help of bees. Birches, poplars, and pines use the wind to bring pollen to their flowers. To make sure this happens, they release enormous quantities of pollen. The pollen is blown by the wind and, with any luck, drifts over to another tree of the same species growing close by. This yellow pollen dust, however, does not only land on other trees. It also lands on cars, windows, sidewalks, and grass.

Another kind of dust is less common. It is blown in on warm winds from the Sahara. The Sahara is the largest desert in the world. It lies in Africa. When the wind blows strongly from the Sahara, it brings sand as fine as dust along with it. This dust can land in places as far away as Europe, the southern United States, and Central and South America. If it lands in your town, cars will look as though they are covered in a fine powder. Plants love dust from the Sahara. For them, it is like fertilizer and it helps them grow.

We've always had pollen and Sahara dust. But today a different kind of dust is drifting over cities—dust made by people. It is called particulate matter and is so fine it is mostly invisible. Particulate matter comes out of the exhaust pipes of vehicles or the chimneys of houses, ships, and factories. Sometimes you can see this gray smog, but when it gets mixed with a lot of air, it disappears from sight. Even when you can't see it, it's bad for you, because it can penetrate deep into your lungs when you breathe it in. That's why some cities in Europe do not allow cars that produce large quantities of particulate matter into their city centers. All cars have a sign on their windshield so the authorities can keep track of them. If you have a yellow sign—or worse, a red one—you have to park outside the city limits. Only cars with green signs are allowed to drive in town. Do you think that would be a good idea in your city?

Particulate matter, however, doesn't just come from gases released into the atmosphere. Take a look at the soles of your shoes. Unless they are brand-new, they will be worn away in places. As you walk, tiny particles are constantly being rubbed off. The same happens with cars. When they are driven, their tires lose tiny pieces of rubber. Tires have to be replaced every few years because the grooves in the treads are no longer deep enough for the tires to grip the road.

Even something as simple as a plastic broom can produce particulate matter. When you sweep, the bristles scratch the floor—and each time they scrape, a little bit of plastic is lost. After a while, you can no longer use the broom because the bristles are too short to do a good job. If you want to do one small thing to help improve air quality, ask your parents to buy a straw broom. The straw will wear away too, but the dust it produces is not harmful, and bacteria and fungi process particles from straw into soil organic matter, just like they process the straw farmers leave lying in the fields.

Toxic plumes of smoke from ships spread for vast distances in the air.

INSIDER INFO

• DUST CATCHERS •

Trees help filter particulate matter out of the air. Fine dust sticks much better to their many leaves and the cracks in their bark than it does to smooth concrete and glass surfaces. This is one of lots of reasons it's good to have as many trees as possible in a city.

Photo Credits

Shutterstock: **6** (backpack) paullos, (containers) anmbph; **7** (hat) Anton Starikov, (magnifying glass) Brian A Jackson; **8** Kimberly Boyles; **10** TFoxFoto; **20** (top) CaseSensitiveFilms, (bottom) Irina999petrova; **22** Lemalisa; **26** Martin Fowler; **27** Belozorova Elena; **28** (top) Keikona, (bottom) alslutsky; **29** (top) Michel VIARD, (bottom) Karel Bock; **41** (bottom) Don Bilski; **42** (bottom right) Eric Isselee; **45** (bottom) LFRabanedo; **46** (top) gavrila bogdan; **58–59** Kenneth Keifer; **62** (left) Naruto_Japan123; **65** Mihai Simonia; **68** Werner Baumgarten; **74** sruilk; **75** Igor Grochev.

iStock: **ii** monkeybusinessimages; **2** AmeliaFox; **4–5** FatCamera; **7** (binoculars) karlowac; **9** Tamas-V; **12** (top) enigma_images; **12–13** (leaves) coffeechcolate, (flowers) Roberto; **16–17** bradleyhebdon; **21** MediaProduction; **23** AHPhotoswpg; **30** BrianLasenby; **36–37** kali9; **38** (left) Goldfinch4ever, (right) Akchamczuk; **39** JasonOndreicka; **41** (top left) skhoward, (top right) ejan Kolar, (middle) ibunt; **44** MychkoAlezander; **47** Hakase; **49** (top) AnnaBreit; **50–51** Halfpoint; **53** brozova;

55 (bottom) WilliamSherman; **56** Kristian_Nilsson; **57** (top) Trever Brolliar, (bottom) suefeldberg; **60** (middle) Carolina Smith; **64** lakshmiprasad S; **69** (bottom) dsafanda; **70** dossyl; **76** kirin_photo.

Jens Steingässer: **3**; **11**; **13** (top); **14–15**; **25** (top and bottom); **25** (middle) **34** (both); **35** (top); **42** (top and bottom); **43** (both); **46** (bottom two); **52**, **54**; **63** (all); **66–67** (all); **69** (top three); **71** (both); **72** (left and right).

Mauritius: **32** Georg Stelzner / imageBROKER; **33** Jack Barr / Alamy; **45** (top) BAO / imageBROKER; **48** Arterra Picture Library / Alamy; **55** (top) Coatsey / Alamy; **60** (top) Ronny Behnert / imageBROKER; **73** Zoonar GmbH / Alamy.

iv nugget16 / Photocase.com; **18** (top) Gavin Rowley / Alamy, (bottom) John Schwarz / Birdpix.com; **24** and **72** (middle) Anja Fischer; **25** (middle) and **40** Jane Billinghurst; **34** (bottom) Peter Wohlleben; **49** (bottom) Jolly Janner; **62** top NASA / JPL-Caltech; **80** Miriam Wohlleben.

Index

HOW TO USE THIS INDEX

This book discusses many facts and topics about nature at home and in the city, like how plants can grow in a sidewalk crack and how bees use electricity. This index will help you quickly find these facts by telling you what pages the facts are on.

To use the index, find the topic you are interested in. The topics are in alphabetical order. The numbers after each topic are the page numbers that you can use to find the information. Page numbers in a range (as in 6–7) means that information is found on both pages 6 *and* 7. Page numbers in **bold** indicate a picture on the page. Sometimes similar information is listed under a different topic. You can find these if you see the words *See also*, and follow the cross-reference to the new topic.

First published in English by Greystone Books in 2023
Originally published in German as *Kommst du mit nach Draußen?*
Eine Entdeckungsreise durch Garten und Stadt © 2021 Verlag
Friedrich Oetinger, Hamburg
Text copyright © 2021 by Peter Wohlleben
English translation copyright © 2023 by Jane Billinghurst

23 24 25 26 27   5 4 3 2 1

Greystone Kids / Greystone Books Ltd.
greystonebooks.com

Cataloguing data available from Library and Archives Canada
ISBN 978-1-77164-895-0 (cloth)
ISBN 978-1-77164-896-7 (epub)

The publisher wishes to thank Carmi Milagros Thompson from
the Florida Museum of Natural History and Maiz Connolly from
the Natural History Museum of Los Angeles County for their
expert reviews of the book.

Editing by Jane Billinghurst
Copy editing by Dawn Loewen
Proofreading by Alison Strobel
Indexing by Stephen Ullstrom
English edition cover, interior design, and illustrations
by Belle Wuthrich
Cover photo by (main) © by DiCon/Photocase.com (main);
Goshlya Sergii/Shutterstock.com (inset)
Photo selection for the English edition by Antonia Banyard

Printed and bound in China on FSC® certified paper by Shenzhen
Reliance Printing. The FSC® label means that materials used for
the product have been responsibly sourced.

Greystone Books thanks the Canada Council for the Arts, the
British Columbia Arts Council, the Province of British Columbia
through the Book Publishing Tax Credit, and the Government of
Canada for supporting our publishing activities.

MIX
Paper from
responsible sources
FSC® C102842

Greystone Books gratefully acknowledges the xʷməθkʷəy̓əm (Musqueam),
Sḵwx̱wú7mesh (Squamish), and səl̓ilwətaɬ (Tsleil-Waututh) peoples on
whose land our Vancouver head office is located.

Peter Wohlleben's books about forests
and conservation have delighted readers
around the world. His children's books
include *Can You Hear the Trees Talking?*,
a young reader's edition of his *New York
Times* bestseller, *The Hidden Life of Trees*,
Do You Know Where the Animals Live?, and the
picture book *Peter and the Tree Children*. He has written
many books for adults including *The Inner Life of Animals*
and *The Secret Wisdom of Nature*.

When he is not writing books, appearing on television
or in movies, or traveling the world talking to people about
trees, Peter can be found at Wohlleben's Forest Academy,
where he leads children on educational tours and works for
the return of primeval forests.